What Was
Pearl Harbor?

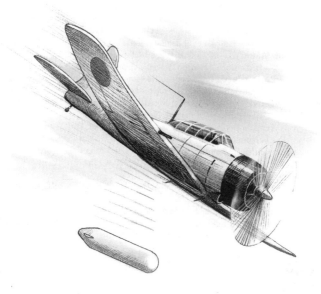

by Patricia Brennan Demuth

illustrated by John Mantha

Grosset & Dunlap
An Imprint of Penguin Group (USA) Inc.

In memory of Uncle Jack Conway, navy man in the
Pacific, and to my beloved Aunt Helen—PBD

For my wife, Leanne —JM

GROSSET & DUNLAP
Published by the Penguin Group
Penguin Group (USA) Inc., 375 Hudson Street, New York, New York 10014, USA
Penguin Group (Canada), 90 Eglinton Avenue East, Suite 700,
Toronto, Ontario M4P 2Y3, Canada (a division of Pearson Penguin Canada Inc.)
Penguin Books Ltd, 80 Strand, London WC2R 0RL, England
Penguin Ireland, 25 St Stephen's Green, Dublin 2, Ireland
(a division of Penguin Books Ltd)
Penguin Group (Australia), 707 Collins Street, Melbourne, Victoria 3008, Australia
(a division of Pearson Australia Group Pty Ltd)
Penguin Books India Pvt Ltd, 11 Community Centre,
Panchsheel Park, New Delhi–110 017, India
Penguin Group (NZ), 67 Apollo Drive, Rosedale, Auckland 0632, New Zealand
(a division of Pearson New Zealand Ltd)
Penguin Books (South Africa), Rosebank Office Park,
181 Jan Smuts Avenue, Parktown North 2193, South Africa
Penguin China, B7 Jiaming Center, 27 East Third Ring Road North,
Chaoyang District, Beijing 100020, China

Penguin Books Ltd, Registered Offices: 80 Strand, London WC2R 0RL, England

Text copyright © 2013 by Patricia Brennan. Illustrations copyright © 2013 by Penguin
Group (USA) Inc. Cover illustration copyright © 2013 by Tim Tomkinson. All rights
reserved. Published by Grosset & Dunlap, a division of Penguin Young Readers Group, 345
Hudson Street, New York, New York 10014. GROSSET & DUNLAP is a trademark of
Penguin Group (USA) Inc. Printed in the U.S.A.

Library of Congress Cataloging-in-Publication Data is available.

ISBN 978-0-448-46462-6 (pbk)   10 9 8 7
ISBN 978-0-448-46580-7 (hc)   10 9 8 7 6 5 4 3 2 1

ALWAYS LEARNING   PEARSON

Contents

What Was Pearl Harbor?

December 7, 1941

It was another bright and beautiful Sunday at Pearl Harbor. Nearly every day was lovely on the Hawaiian island of Oahu.

In 1941, Pearl Harbor was home to a giant military base. Altogether, eighteen thousand US Navy and US Army men were based there. More than one hundred warships docked at the harbor. The fleet included eight massive battleships, armored and armed to the hilt. Most of them stretched the length of two football fields. There were airfields scattered around the island, too, filled with hundreds of American warplanes.

The American sailors and airmen were training hard in case the United States joined World War

II. The war, however, seemed far away. All the fighting was in Europe and Africa.

The only threat in the Pacific was from Japan. Lately, tensions had grown between Japan and America. But peace talks were underway. So on this December morning, the men at Pearl Harbor were thinking about their Sunday plans, not war.

At 7:55 a.m. sailors on every ship were getting ready to raise the flag. Aboard the battleship *Nevada,* a navy band lined up to play "The Star Spangled Banner." Some of the band members saw planes in the distance. They were flying low to the ground. It seemed odd, but the men thought little of it. US pilots were probably having drills.

The planes, however, kept coming straight toward the harbor. That was even odder. Some in the band started to feel nervous. What was going on?

Then, just as the band began playing, fighter planes flew directly over the harbor . . . and they started dropping bombs!

One plane dove over the *Nevada* and started spraying the band with bullets. The band saw a red sun on its wings, the symbol of Japan. All doubts vanished: This was a Japanese attack!

For just a moment, the players lost the beat. But they refused to stop in the middle of their national anthem. They played to the end—then raced for cover! Amazingly, no bullets hit them.

Thousands of others were not so lucky. All around the *Nevada*, American sailors were dying as battleships exploded.

The Japanese were hammering Pearl Harbor in an air attack. They had caught the United States by complete surprise. By the time the attack ended a couple of hours later, 2,402 Americans were dead.

The events of that day plunged the United States into World War II, a war that would not end until the summer of 1945.

December 7, 1941, at Pearl Harbor became a
day burned forever into America's memory.

Pearl Harbor

Pearl Harbor is on the island of Oahu, Hawaii. (At the time of the attack, Hawaii was a US territory. It would become the fiftieth US state in 1959.) Besides the harbor itself, there were shipyards, airfields, power plants, barracks, office buildings, and a navy hospital with a thousand beds.

In the middle of the harbor was Ford Island. Seven battleships—the pride of the US Pacific Fleet—were anchored together on the eastern side of the island, lined up neatly in what was called Battleship Row. These ships were the *Arizona, California, Maryland, Nevada, Oklahoma, Tennessee,* and *West Virginia.* On the day of the attack, a repair ship called the *Vestal* was also there, moored beside the *Arizona.* The battleship *Pennsylvania* was dry-docked nearby.

Battleship Row was the prime target of Japanese torpedo pilots.

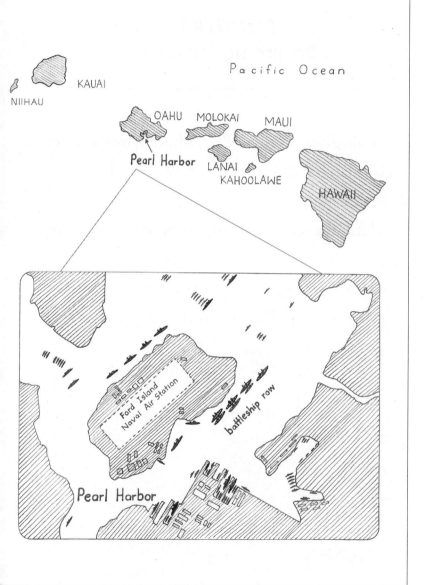

Pacific Ocean

NIIHAU

KAUAI

OAHU   MOLOKAI   MAUI

Pearl Harbor

LANAI

KAHOOLAWE

HAWAII

Ford Island
Naval Air Station

battleship row

Pearl Harbor

9

CHAPTER 1
Becoming Enemies

While bombs fell on Pearl Harbor, one seaman exclaimed, "I didn't even know [the Japanese] were sore at us!"

Until the attack, many Americans had not realized that Japan and America were becoming bitter enemies. The enemy on most people's minds was Adolf Hitler. Hitler was the ruthless dictator

of Nazi Germany. His aim was to conquer all the democracies of Europe.

In 1939, Hitler had started World War II when his troops stormed into Poland. Immediately, Britain and France declared war on Germany.

The Nazis crushed one country after another. In the spring of 1940, the Netherlands and France fell. That left England to stand alone against the Germans.

President Franklin Roosevelt shipped arms, tanks, and planes to help the British. But he did not send American soldiers.

Franklin Delano Roosevelt
(1882-1945)

US President Franklin Roosevelt led America through two deeply trying times: the Great Depression and World War II.

Roosevelt was born in Hyde Park, New York, in 1882. He came from a rich family and wanted to devote his life to public service. At just twenty-eight, he won a seat in the US Senate. And during World War I, he served as assistant secretary of the navy.

In 1921, tragedy struck. Roosevelt fell ill with polio. It crippled his legs and left him unable to walk. Few people thought he could stay in politics. But Roosevelt fought back with the help of his wife, Eleanor. He was governor of New York from 1929 to 1932.

Roosevelt was first elected president in 1932. The country was in the grip of the Great Depression, which had left millions of Americans jobless. An inspiring speaker, Roosevelt told Americans that "the only thing we have to fear is fear itself." He created jobs programs that in time helped America get back on its feet.

Roosevelt was elected president three more times—in 1936, 1940, and 1944. (Because of a 1951 change to the Constitution, now no one can be elected president for more than two terms.) When Roosevelt began his third term, World War II was

already raging in Europe. At first, Roosevelt promised to keep America out of the war. After the Pearl Harbor attack, however, that changed.

Roosevelt died on April 12, 1945. Less than a month later, Germany surrendered. Japan then surrendered on September 2, 1945.

Most Americans wanted to stay out of the war. World War I, which had ended in 1918, was still fresh in their minds. America had lost over a hundred thousand soldiers then. It was supposed to be the "war to end all wars." But just twenty years later, another world war had started.

On the other side of the earth, another military power was also on the move.

Japan is a nation made up of many islands, surrounded by thousands of miles of Pacific Ocean. For thousands of years, Japan had kept apart from the rest of the world. Then, in 1853, Japan opened its doors to world trade. Swiftly, its society became modern. Its military grew powerful. Japan began to dream of becoming a world power.

However, the small nation didn't have the resources to meet its goals. It needed coal, rubber, and oil. In the 1930s, Japan set out to get these resources by conquering its neighbors in Asia and the Pacific.

JAPAN

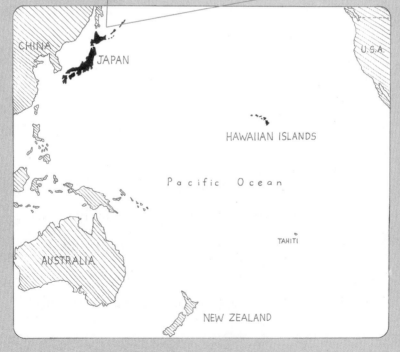

CHINA

JAPAN

U.S.A.

HAWAIIAN ISLANDS

Pacific Ocean

TAHITI

AUSTRALIA

NEW ZEALAND

In 1937, Japan invaded China and set off a
full-scale war. By 1940, Japan was ready to seize
lands in the South Pacific, including present-day
Indonesia, Malaysia, Vietnam, Cambodia, and
the Philippines. Back then European countries

ruled most of these lands. But they were caught up in the war with Hitler. Only one power stood in Japan's way: the United States.

In June 1940, Japan boldly invaded French Indochina (present-day Vietnam and Cambodia). Roosevelt took action. He moved the US Pacific Fleet from California to Pearl Harbor in Hawaii. Now a powerful US force stood guard in the Pacific against further Japanese advances.

Three months later, Japan signed a pact to join forces with Nazi Germany and its ally, Italy. Japan was sending a clear message to the United States: Back off.

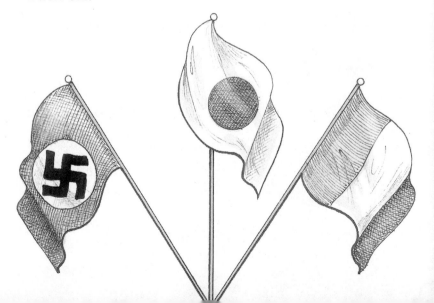

Throughout 1941, messages went back and forth between America and the military leaders in control of Japan. America insisted that Japan withdraw from Indochina and stop its takeovers. Japan insisted that the United States should mind its own business—Japan was free to do what it wanted.

By summer, President Roosevelt slapped a trade embargo on Japan. This meant that Japan could no longer get US oil. For Japan, this was grim indeed. The country depended on American oil. Without it, Japan's military machine would grind to a halt.

Japan was faced with two choices: It could agree to American demands, or it could go to war against the United States.

Prime Minister Tojo

Emperor Hirohito
(1901–1989)

In 1941, Hirohito was emperor of Japan. "Emperor" makes it sound as if he were powerful. However, the government was actually run by military chiefs and the prime minister. Hirohito wanted to keep peace with the United States. In the end, however, he approved the attack on Pearl Harbor.

Four years later, in 1945, Hirohito went on the radio to broadcast Japan's surrender. It was the first time his people had ever heard his voice. He died in 1989 after a sixty-two-year reign.

CHAPTER 2
A Dangerous and Risky Plan

As tensions rose between Japan and the United States, some American leaders feared a Japanese attack somewhere in the Pacific, probably in the Philippines. Almost no one thought the Japanese would dare to attack Pearl Harbor.

Three things seemed to make Pearl Harbor attack-proof. One, the mighty Pacific Fleet was based there. Surely any attack would be crushed right away. Two, torpedoes could not be used there. Torpedoes were cigar-shaped missiles dropped from airplanes. They fired into the hulls of ships below the waterline. The waters of Pearl Harbor, however, were shallow. Torpedoes would get stuck in the mud and fail to explode. Three, Pearl Harbor was four thousand miles from Japan.

A surprise attack seemed impossible. Planes or ships would certainly be spotted long before they could strike.

The Japanese understood these dangers. Most of their military leaders discarded the idea of attacking Pearl Harbor—all except one. He was Admiral Isoroku Yamamoto, an important officer in the Imperial Navy.

Admiral Yamamoto did not believe that Japan could win a long war against the United States. He had lived in America for several years and had seen the power of its economy and military up close. Nonetheless, Yamamoto did think that Japan could win an all-important first strike against the United States—*if* it came as a surprise.

A first strike at Pearl Harbor could deal a crushing blow to the US fleet. America would not be able to strike back for many months. In the meantime, Japan would be free to take over the South Pacific. That would "break the enemy's will to fight," Yamamoto said.

Yamamoto's idea was dangerous and risky. Nonetheless, the military gave him the go-ahead to put a plan together.

Yamamoto gathered a team of engineers and military leaders. They came up with a very different kind of attack plan, something that had never been tried before.

Up until then, great naval battles were fought in the open sea. Huge battleships pounded each other with warheads shot from cannons. But in Yamamoto's plan, the attack would come from the air. Planes would take off from huge aircraft carriers.

An aircraft carrier is basically a floating airport. It can transport hundreds of airplanes across the seas. The long, flat upper deck on a carrier provides a runway for takeoffs and landings.

Yamamoto's master plan called for several carriers to bring hundreds of planes within flying distance of Pearl Harbor. The strike force would include bombers and fighter planes. And the key weapon would be a torpedo. A torpedo that worked in shallow water.

Yamamoto's team came up with the smart idea of putting wooden fins on torpedoes. The fins would make the torpedo turn toward a target almost as soon as it hit the water. With the torpedo problem solved, the Japanese now could rip gashes into the hulls of US battleships and destroy them.

Admiral Isoroku Yamamoto
(1884–1943)

Fifty-seven-year-old Admiral Yamamoto was the mastermind behind the Pearl Harbor attack. Yamamoto lived for a while in the United States— first as a student at Harvard University and later as a Japanese official in Washington, DC. During those

years, he developed a deep respect for America. When World War II broke out, he had concerns about Japan siding with Germany. He thought it would lead to a war with the United States—a war that Japan could not win.

Yamamoto believed airpower was the way to win wars now. He even foresaw that sea battles could be won by firing at ships from the air. (Before, battles at sea meant big ships fighting against other big ships.) Yamamoto oversaw the building of a massive air fleet in Japan. By 1941, the Japanese had nearly five thousand warplanes. His planning for the Pearl Harbor attack proved to be brilliant.

Yamamoto was tracked and killed by US Army troops in 1943 for his part in the attack on Pearl Harbor.

CHAPTER 3
Top Secret

The attack was top secret right from the start.

Japanese fighter pilots had months of training. But they didn't know what they were training for. They were kept in the dark until right before the attack was set in motion.

Very few in the Japanese military knew about the plan, either. For many months, not even Emperor Hirohito was told. Neither was the mild-mannered Japanese ambassador in Washington, DC. He learned about the attack *after* it happened.

By mid-November, the Japanese fleet was ready to depart. But how could giant aircraft carriers leave Japan without being seen by US spies?

The answer: They did not leave in a group. The warships began leaving Japan one at a time, going

by separate routes to escape attention. Eventually, all the ships would meet up at a remote island north of Japan.

Destroyer

Battleship

The route was through rough, icy seas. This made it less likely that they'd be spotted by ships from other countries. Radios were turned off. Now US Navy planes could not pick up their signals. Oil tankers chugged behind the fleet so

Tanker

Aircraft Carrier

Submarine

that the warships never had to stop in ports to refuel. The Japanese fleet numbered some thirty ships in all. There were six aircraft carriers bearing hundreds of warplanes. The other ships came along to protect the carriers or refuel them.

There was also a fleet of submarines in the convoy. The submarines were the only vessels that would be going all the way to Pearl Harbor. Five of the submarines carried midget subs. Before dawn on the day of the attack, the midgets were supposed to slip inside the harbor. They would lie on the dark harbor bottom until the bombing

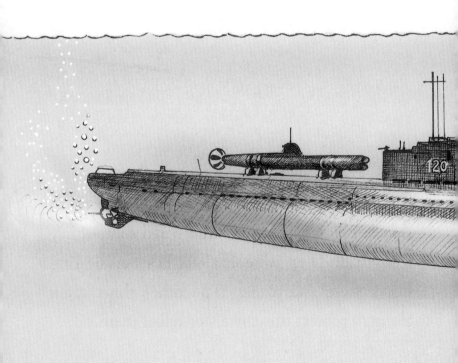

began. Then the tiny subs would open fire, attacking the US ships from underwater.

The commander in charge of the ships at sea was Vice Admiral Nagumo. He knew that there was a chance the attack could still be called off. If Japan and the United States reached an agreement, his orders were to "return to the homeland."

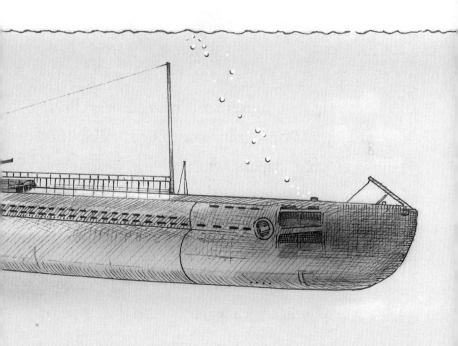

Admiral Nagumo

However, an agreement seemed less likely every day. Washington continued talks, not knowing that Japan was talking peace and planning war. President Roosevelt offered to lift the trade embargo if Japan withdrew its troops from Indochina.

That idea made Japan furious. On December 1, Japanese military leaders met with the emperor to urge him to go to war. Prime Minister Tojo grimly reported, "Matters have reached the point where Japan must begin war . . . to preserve her Empire." The emperor agreed.

The next day, Nagumo received a message. "Climb Mt. Niitaka," it said. Mt. Niitaka was the highest mountain in the Japanese empire. The message was a secret way of saying, "Proceed! Attack Pearl Harbor!"

CHAPTER 4
Trouble at Dawn

While most people at Pearl Harbor were sleeping, Commander Mitsuo Fuchida prepared for battle. Fuchida donned a red shirt. If bullets hit him, the shirt would hide signs of blood from his troops.

The Japanese fleet had stopped 230 miles north of Hawaii. From this spot, attack planes would take off from the carriers in two waves, an hour apart.

Fuchida saw with alarm that the seas were very rough—dangerous for takeoff. Water burst over the decks of the carriers, which rocked back and forth. Crews desperately hung to the planes on deck to stop from falling overboard. But the day of battle had come. There was no turning back.

Shortly after 6:00 a.m., Fuchida gave the order to take off. One by one, airplanes from all six carriers roared into the sky. The pilots circled until 183 planes were in the air. Fuchida was in the lead plane. The other pilots followed behind him. Pearl Harbor was ninety minutes away.

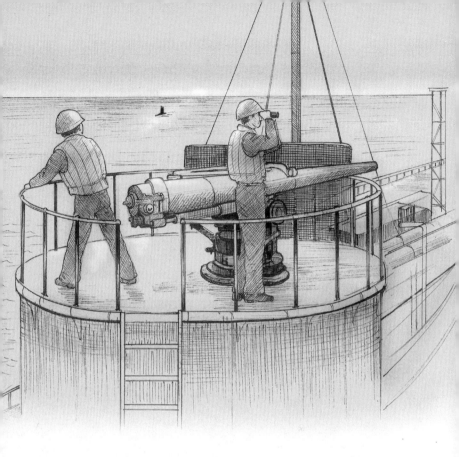

At Oahu, a small ship called the USS *Ward* was on early-morning patrol near the entrance to Pearl Harbor. At 6:45, lookouts suddenly spotted something sticking out of the water. It looked like a buoy—but it wasn't. It was the conning tower of an enemy submarine!

"Commence firing!" the patrol boat commander ordered. His crew fired at the sub, first with guns and then with depth charges (underwater bombs). The submarine exploded in a gush of foam. Although they did not know it then, the sailors had just sunk a Japanese midget submarine.

Without delay, the commander radioed in a report of the sinking. The message went slowly

from one office to the next. Finally it reached top headquarters. The report "caused quite a stir," said one witness. However, officers thought it was not "important enough to put the whole fleet on alert." No action was taken.

Another danger sign quickly followed at 7:02. Two young privates were on duty at a lonely radar station on the northern tip of Oahu. Suddenly a

huge blip appeared on the radar screen. It looked like a group of fifty or more planes was just 140 miles away!

One of the soldiers grabbed the phone and reported the sighting. An officer listened to the news. But he remembered that several US planes were due in that morning from California. He figured those planes accounted for the blip on the radar screen. "Don't worry about it," he said.

Twice danger signals were spotted. Twice they

were ignored. Later, the military would deeply regret those mistakes.

Meanwhile, the first wave of Japanese fighter planes drew steadily closer to Oahu. By 7:30, the second wave of planes was also in the air. Altogether, there were 353 enemy planes! Everything was going according to plan. Still, Commander Fuchida had reason to worry. A cloud cover lay over the island.

That would make it hard for his pilots to find their targets. Then, suddenly, the clouds broke. The coast appeared below. It would be a clear day after all, perfect for an air attack.

Fuchida saw the US battleships up ahead. "A more favorable situation could not have been imagined," he later wrote.

Fuchida radioed his pilots. *"To! To! To!"* (Attack! Attack! Attack!) It was 7:49 a.m.

Japanese Navy Type 97 Carrier Attack Plane

A Japanese bomber approaching Pearl Harbor

Franklin Delano Roosevelt

Hideki Tojo

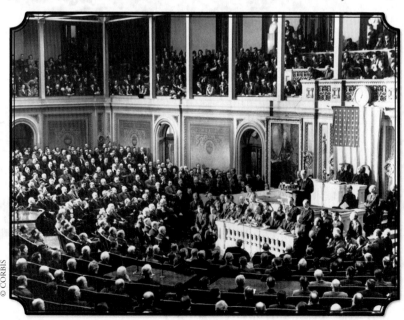

President Roosevelt requesting a declaration of
war from Congress on December 8, 1941

A Japanese commanding officer on one of the aircraft carriers

Aerial photograph of Pearl
Harbor, Hawaii

Hirohito,
emperor of Japan

Japanese planes take off from aircraft carrier to attack Pearl Harbor

US sailors dousing flames on the USS *West Virginia*

Aerial view of "Battleship Row" at the beginning of the bombing

2nd Lieutenant Kenneth M. Taylor (left) and
2nd Lieutenant George S. Welch (right)

A slightly damaged USS Maryland and the
capsized USS Oklahoma

Newspapers announce Japanese
relocation to internment camps

Poster in remembrance of the
attack on Pearl Harbor

A World War II Japanese "long lance"
torpedo, outside US Navy headquarters

Memorial plaque mounted on the
wreck of the battleship USS Utah

Sailors honoring men killed in the attack on Naval Air Station

USS Arizona sunk and burning as men aboard USS Tennessee

(left) aim hoses at the water to deflect oil from their ship

Torpedo planes attacking "Battleship Row"

Unit 22 Band of the USS Arizona on the night before the attack

A New York crowd holding up newspapers
announcing the Japanese attack on Pearl Harbor

USS Arizona Memorial

Naval History & Heritage Command, Washington Navy Yard, DC

USS Indianapolis commanding officer, Captain E. W. Hanson
(second from right), and men

Library of Congress, Prints & Photographs Division

The Manzanar Relocation Center in California

Doris Miller (right) receiving
the Navy Cross

Honolulu, Hawaii, in the 1940s

A crashed Japanese Type 00 Carrier Fighter ("Zero")

Typical sleeping quarters of US Navy men on a battleship

Japanese naval officer giving troops instructions

All forty torpedo bombers flew toward the US battleships. Behind them were high-level bombers. Other groups of planes tore off to the airfields.

Fuchida scanned the skies. All he saw were his own planes. No American aircraft were rushing to defend the Pacific Fleet.

"Tora! Tora! Tora!" Fuchida radioed the Japanese Navy. (Tiger! Tiger! Tiger!) The code word meant that they had made it into the harbor in secret. So far, so good.

Way of the Warrior

Before Japanese troops left for Pearl Harbor, Yamamoto reminded them to stay true to their Bushido code. This ancient code laid out strict rules of conduct for warriors. They had to be loyal, do their duty, show courage and self-control, and be ready to die for Japan. Bushido warriors valued honor over their own lives.

Bushido warriors always wore certain items of clothing in battle. On the morning of December 7, pilots tied scarves around their heads. On each scarf was a flaming red dot. It stood for the Rising Sun, which was the symbol of Japan. The Japanese word for "certain victory" was sewn into each scarf. Around their waists some of the pilots tied a "belt of a thousand stitches" for good luck. The belts were made by Japanese women, each sewing one stitch until there were a thousand.

CHAPTER 5
"This Is No Drill!"

A quiet calm lay over Pearl Harbor that Sunday morning. Many sailors were sleeping in late. Many others were chowing down in mess halls.

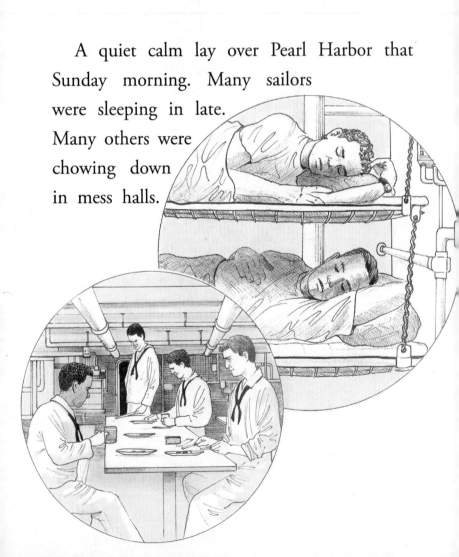

Some were heading ashore for their day off. The huge battleships lay peacefully at anchor, waves lapping gently at their giant hulls.

Then fighter planes, thick as hornets, darkened the sky.

Yet few people were worried—at least at first. They figured that US pilots were on a practice drill or putting on an air show.

Even the sight of bombs did not alarm one admiral. *What a stupid, careless pilot!* he said to himself when he saw a bomb drop from a plane. He too was sure that this was only a drill.

Another officer thought a pilot was showing off when his plane swooped in very low. He looked for the reckless pilot's number—and saw instead a red ball on the plane's wing! It was the symbol of Japan!

At home, Admiral Kimmel had just put on his starched white uniform when he heard a distant boom. Running outside, he saw pillars of smoke and fire rising from Pearl Harbor! Overhead, flocks of airplanes streaked by. Kimmel took one look at the red dots on their wings and the awful truth became clear: The Japanese were attacking! The admiral turned "as white as his uniform," said a neighbor.

Kimmel dashed off to send the alarm: "This is no drill! Man your stations!"

In the harbor, loudspeakers on the US warships blared, "Real planes! Real bombs!" On every deck, sailors yelled to their mates, "Japanese attack!"

This is not a drill!

Real planes!

Real bombs!

Japanese planes stormed in first, screaming low over the harbor. They let loose deadly torpedoes that shot through the water like sea monsters. Underwater, the warheads went straight toward the hulls of the big ships.

One after another, the US ships reeled under attack. The ships seemed to "explode in a chain reaction," said one eyewitness. A day that started with quiet calm had become a nightmare.

Japanese Attack Planes

The Japanese had different warplanes to do different jobs.

Fighter planes were nicknamed Zeroes. They could dive low to the ground, firing machine guns located in their wings. Zeroes could veer and turn with dizzying speed. None of the US planes at that time could move with the speed and ease of the Zeroes.

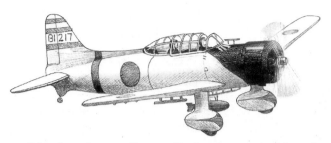

Dive bombers, often called Vals, carried bombs under both wings and one huge bomb on their underside. They could swoop in low to hit their targets with true aim.

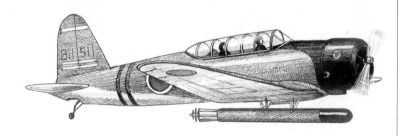

High-altitude bombers, called Kates, dropped 1,700-pound bombs from high in the sky. The bombs gathered force as they plunged to earth. Other Kates dropped the special torpedoes that had been made for Pearl Harbor's shallow waters.

CHAPTER 6
Fifteen Minutes of Terror

The attack began at 7:55. The next fifteen minutes were the most deadly.

On board the US ships, chaos ruled. Bombs killed many sailors instantly. The wounded struggled to get to battle stations and fight back. They raced over decks slick with blood and oil. Water gushed into gaping holes in the ships. On lower decks, men were trapped in flooded rooms.

In only fifteen minutes, the Japanese managed to carry out most of the destruction at Pearl Harbor.

It was 8:05 when the *Oklahoma* on Battleship Row took the first of seven torpedoes. With gashes on its sides, the ship was thrown into pitch blackness. Seawater poured in, and the *Oklahoma* began to sink. Seamen were trapped below in the darkness. "I was tossed and spun around, pitched into a great nothingness," said one survivor. "All of us—the living, dying, and the dead—were whirled around together."

"Slowly, sickeningly, the *Oklahoma* began to roll over on her side," said a witness. Within minutes, only its rounded hull showed above water. It looked like a huge dead whale. The *Oklahoma* hit the bottom of the harbor just

eight minutes after the first torpedo strike. Four
hundred men died aboard the ship.

At the same time, a torpedo blasted directly underneath the *West Virginia* and sent the crew flying. The huge warship began to topple at once. Two more torpedoes capsized the *Utah*. Another split open the hull of a smaller ship called the *Oglala,* which would capsize two hours later.

"It was awful. Great ships were dying before my eyes," said an eyewitness.

As US ships were exploding, so were US planes. Japanese bomber planes attacked nearby airfields with fury. Their goal was to destroy planes on the ground before American pilots could get in them and fight back.

The first air bases attacked were Hickam, Wheeler, Bellows, and Ewa. The planes at each were lined up close together, wingtip to wingtip. They had been parked together out in the open so they could be easily guarded from spies. Tragically, they were now wide-open to attack.

In the first fifteen minutes of the attack at Ewa, thirty-three of the forty-nine planes on the field were destroyed, with the remaining sixteen too damaged to fly.

Nearby at Wheeler, bombers killed hundreds of soldiers in their barracks, many of them still

sleeping. At Hickam, a bomb took out dozens of planes in one shattering blast. "Dive bombers were tearing the place to pieces," a witness said.

But the worst was yet to come. And the mighty *Arizona* battleship would be target.

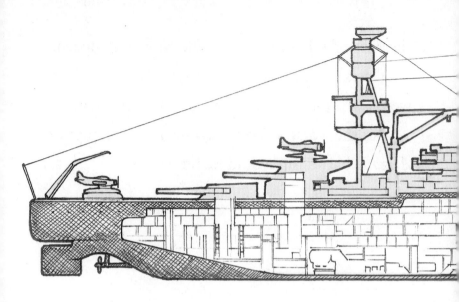

The huge USS *Arizona* was home to fifteen hundred officers and sailors. Living there was more like living in a city than on a ship. Its giant hull was six hundred feet long. Thick armor covered the top decks of the ship. Heavy weapons and a highly trained crew protected it. Ammunition was stored in a hold belowdecks.

For the first several minutes of the attack, the *Arizona* was able to withstand the torpedo hits.

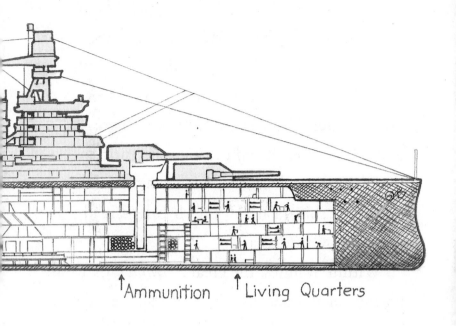

↑Ammunition ↑Living Quarters

At 8:10, her mast still stood tall. Then a bomb came hurtling down from ten thousand feet overhead. It pierced the *Arizona's* thick armor, blasted through its decks, and blew up in the hold where all the ammunition was stored. More than one million pounds of gunpowder exploded in a towering fireball.

In that single moment, over one thousand men on the *Arizona* were killed.

Stunned witnesses saw fire shooting five hundred feet into the air. Bodies flew in the sky. The *Arizona* itself bolted several feet off the water. Then it simply broke in two. Shockwaves shuddered through the entire island, tossing dozens of men overboard on nearby ships. Parts of the *Arizona* rained down all over the island.

Within minutes, the great *Arizona* sank to the bottom of the harbor. There it still lies. The bodies of the dead were never recovered.

Many of the victims from the *Arizona* were brothers. Thirty-seven sets of brothers had been serving together on the ship. Only one set of brothers survived. After the attack on Pearl Harbor, the United States tried never to assign brothers to the same ship.

The USS *Arizona*

Before the attack, one sailor on the *Arizona* wrote home saying, "Well, Mother, a battleship is about as safe a vessel as you can find in a fleet, so you don't have to worry."

Giant guns were mounted around the sides of the *Arizona*. It took sixteen men to work each one. The fifty-foot barrels spewed out warheads that

weighed as much as 1,500 pounds and that could hit ships twenty miles away.

The *Arizona* crews were prepared for a battle at sea. But the Pearl Harbor attack came from the air. Most of the huge guns on the *Arizona* never had a chance to fire.

Nearly half of all those who died at Pearl Harbor died on the *Arizona*.

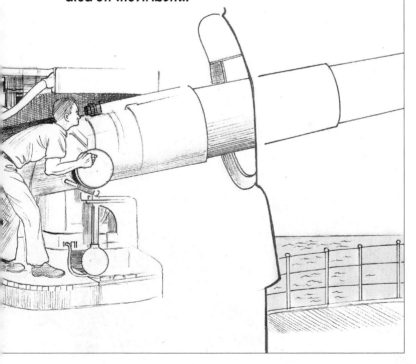

CHAPTER 7
A Sea on Fire

Oil pouring out of the dying US ships covered the water in a thick slime that caught fire. Sailors jumping off burning ships landed in water that was burning, too.

Meanwhile, the US airfields were also ablaze as fuel exploded from bombed planes.

Japanese bomber planes did not stop hammering the bases until every weapon in their loads had been used.

Fighter planes swooped in behind the bombers. They blasted the bases with machine guns. Flying low to the ground, they fired at everything in sight—planes, barracks, dining halls, and men running for safety. Soldiers saw Japanese pilots lean out of their cockpits and smile as they streaked past. The planes flew "so close it looked like you could throw rocks at them," said an airman.

At 8:35 there was a brief pause in the action as the first wave of Japanese planes flew off.

About twenty minutes later, a second wave of 170 Japanese planes roared into Pearl Harbor to finish the job by destroying the ships that had already been hit and the planes that were already burning.

But now the Americans were ready to fight back. Soldiers and sailors raced to arm the big guns and clear the runways and decks. Most of the twenty-nine enemy planes that US forces downed that day were destroyed during the second-wave attack.

By 9:45 a.m., the skies were empty. The attack was over. Less than two hours had passed since the first bombs fell.

The Japanese pilots flew back to their carriers. They had won a stunning victory and paid little for it. They lost only twenty-nine out of 353 planes in the raid. None of their six aircraft carriers had even been discovered, let alone harmed.

By a stroke of luck, the United States hadn't lost any aircraft carriers, either. None of the three US carriers in the Pacific Fleet was at Pearl Harbor that day.

The US losses, however, were staggering. More than 2,400 Americans were killed. Almost 1,200 were wounded. The US Pacific Fleet had been shattered. Twenty-one vessels were sunk or damaged, including all eight of the great battleships at Pearl Harbor. Out of nearly four hundred aircraft on the island, only seventy-one were left unharmed.

The Japanese had kept Yamamoto's promise. They had dealt a "crushing blow" to the US Pacific force. Pearl Harbor lay in smoking ruins.

CHAPTER 8
Bravery against All Odds

In the middle of an attack, countless American sailors and soldiers fought back as best they could.

Crews who got to their battle stations remained fighting until the very last minute. Commander Cassin Young was in charge of a repair ship named the *Vestal* when the first bombs hit. Young dashed to the bridge and started firing one of the big guns. Even though he was blown overboard, Young managed to swim back to his ship.

Fires were burning on board. Intense heat and flames blasted from the *Arizona*, parked alongside the *Vestal*. And more bombs were still dropping. But Young and his men succeeded in moving their ship away from the *Arizona* and beaching it so it wouldn't sink.

Split-second decisions had to be made in the rage of battle. Dorie Miller, a Navy cook on the *West Virginia,* ended up on the ship's bridge beside an antiaircraft gun. It was a powerful weapon built to return enemy fire. Miller had not been trained to use the huge gunner. He was African American. Shamefully, at that time African Americans were not trained for combat. Miller grabbed the gun anyway, pulled the trigger, and started firing at enemy planes.

The quick action of men like Miller surprised the Japanese. From the air, Commander Fuchida was "startled" to see gunfire returned from US battleships "less than five minutes after the first bomb had fallen."

A sailor named Carl Carson, who had escaped from the *Arizona,* passed out as he swam to shore in the burning water. Another sailor rescued him. But Carson refused to sit onshore and recover. Instead he answered a bugler's call for help on the *Tennessee.* He went to that ship's battle station, which was located at the same place on the *Tennessee* as it was on the *Arizona.*

At the air bases, US soldiers reacted swiftly, too. They were unable to use the antiaircraft guns because the ammunition had been locked away for protection. So they fought back with whatever weapons they could find. Some entered the smoking cockpits of damaged planes, ripped out the machine guns, and started firing them at the enemy in the sky. One soldier was able to down a low-flying Japanese plane using a rifle.

At Kaneohe airfield, airman John Finn broke into an ammunition truck and passed out machine guns and rifles to other soldiers. Finn started firing a machine gun from a training platform in the middle of the field. Zeroes dove low to the ground, gunning for him. But Finn wouldn't budge. Even while wounded, he kept fighting back. "Our hangars were burning, our planes were exploding where they sat, and men were dying," Finn recalled later. "I was so mad, I didn't have time to be afraid."

CHAPTER 9
Coming to the Rescue

The destroyed planes meant that almost all of the American pilots were grounded. But young pilots George Welch and Kenneth Taylor fought their way into the sky. The two were friends.

When the first bombs hit, Welch and Taylor were talking about going for a swim. They had been out all night dancing and playing cards.

Suddenly, they heard a blast. Seconds later, Zeroes zoomed overhead. They both saw the Rising Sun under the wings.

In Taylor's car, they tore off to Haleiwa airfield. The Japanese had not reached it yet. At the airfield, the pilots wasted no time. They jumped inside their cockpits and soared off, straight into a buzz saw of enemy planes. They were still in tuxedoes!

Welch and Taylor were vastly outnumbered. But for an hour and a half, they chased Japanese planes in the sky, diving and swooping to avoid hits or to get a better aim. At one point, Welch rescued his buddy Taylor, who was being fired on by an enemy plane at his tail.

Twice the young pilots landed to refuel and rearm. Twice they flew back into the battle. American soldiers on the ground cheered at the sight of aircraft with the US flag. It was one of the few things to cheer about that morning.

Taylor and Welch returned safely to the base. They are believed to have shot down seven enemy planes, about one fourth of all Japanese planes downed that day.

While some brave men were fighting back, others worked to save the lives of wounded Americans. Rescue boats threaded their way about the burning harbor to pull half-dead victims from the water. Bullets from strafing Japanese planes did not stop them.

On the *Arizona*, sailor John Anderson was knocked out cold when his ship exploded. As soon as he came to, he helped lower wounded mates into a lifeboat. Once onshore, Anderson did not want to stay where it was safe. He found a boat and rescued men in the harbor who were severely burned and black with oil.

Onshore, citizens helped military doctors and nurses with the wounded. The work went on for days. Makeshift hospitals sprung up across the island—on lawns, in barracks, in schools, even in airplane hangars. "Every table in the mess hall had a man on it," said one sailor.

In one school, doctors operated on tables in the cafeteria. As night fell on December 7, thick

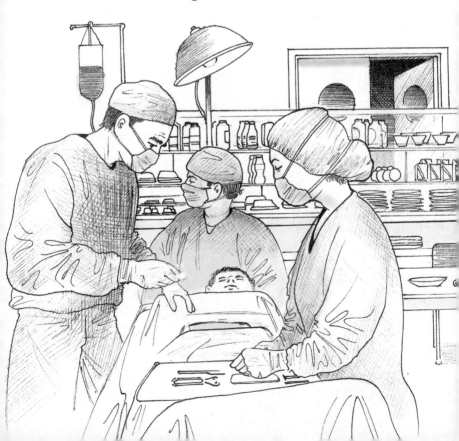

smoke covered the harbor. A sense of shock gripped the island. Mrs. Earle, Admiral Kimmel's neighbor, summed up the feeling: "Even as I watched it happen I was unable to believe the unbelievable."

CHAPTER 10
Joining the War

Yamamoto expected his attack to "break the enemy's will to fight." He was wrong. Just the opposite happened.

Doubts about entering World War II disappeared instantly. The United States had been attacked. Now the war had come home to Americans.

On December 8 in the Capitol building, President Roosevelt addressed Congress. "Yesterday, December 7, 1941—a date which will live in infamy," he began, "the United States was suddenly and deliberately attacked by naval and air forces of the Empire of Japan. The United States was at peace with that nation."

Millions of Americans heard the news on the radio. The president's words spoke to the heart of America's anger. Americans thought it was dishonorable for Japan to attack without first declaring war. And it was unthinkable that Japan would make war while talking peace.

The president asked Congress to declare war against Japan. They answered with a resounding *yes.* The United States would also join forces with the Allies to fight the Nazis.

Tens of thousands of men enlisted in the service. Women stepped up to fill their jobs at home. American factories worked for the war effort.

Japanese American Camps

In the United States, feelings of anger and suspicion against the Japanese ran high after Pearl Harbor. Two months after the attack, President Roosevelt made a terrible decision. He ordered all Japanese Americans living on the West Coast to be

put in prison camps. More than 110,000 innocent people were forced to live behind barbed wire for the rest of the war. Two-thirds of them had been born in the United States. No one in the camps was ever found guilty of wrongdoing. They were loyal US citizens.

In 1988, the US government finally apologized to all Japanese Americans for this tragedy. Money was sent to those who were kept in camps. And a fund was set up to teach the lessons of this shameful affair.

By the end of World War II, factory workers had made almost 300,000 new planes and more than 2,500 ships!

The Pacific Fleet was restored. Six of the eight bombed battleships at Pearl Harbor were repaired and put back into service.

After the Pearl Harbor attack, Japan seized more lands in Southeast Asia and the Pacific. But in June 1942, America won an important battle against Japan at the island of Midway. Four of Japan's six aircraft carriers were destroyed. After that, the tide started to turn against Japan.

In Europe, the fighting finally ended in May 1945. Germany surrendered but the Japanese had not.

America wanted the war to be over. So, on August 6, 1945, the new US president, Harry Truman, gave the order to drop an atomic bomb on the Japanese city of Hiroshima. Three days later, another was dropped on Nagasaki.

CHINA

RUSSIA

Sea of Japan

KOREA

JAPAN

Hiroshima

Nagasaki

Pacific Ocean

These bombs were like no weapons the world had ever seen. Think of how much bigger a basketball is than a pea and you will have some

idea of how much more powerful an atom bomb is next to a regular bomb. In an instant, whole neighborhoods disappeared. Only one building was left standing in Hiroshima. In an instant, a quarter of a million Japanese citizens were killed—men, women, and children. They were not soldiers; they were just ordinary people.

President
Harry S. Truman

Six days after the bombing of Nagasaki, the Japanese surrendered. World War II came to a bitter end.

Was Truman's decision to drop atomic bombs on Japan the right thing to do?

That question has been debated since 1945. Yes, it ended the war. But what about wars in the future? Now enemies had the power to wipe each other off the face of the earth. Since 1945, peace efforts around the world have worked to make sure atomic bombs are never used again.

All told, from the onset of World War II in 1939 to its end, fifty to seventy million people died. More than four hundred thousand were American. For the United States, World War II started on that sunny Sunday at Pearl Harbor.

The broken hull of the *Arizona* is now the site of a war memorial. Each year, one and a half million visitors board boats to view the sunken remains of the ship in the clear blue harbor water. They come to honor the 1,177 men whose bodies are still inside the *Arizona*.

Many of the visitors to the memorial are Japanese. Today Japan and America are close friends and strong allies. Both sides suffered

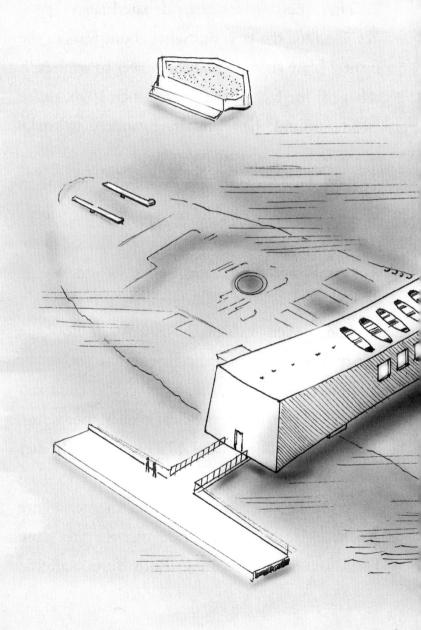

terribly in the war. The memory of that war now
binds both countries together in peace.

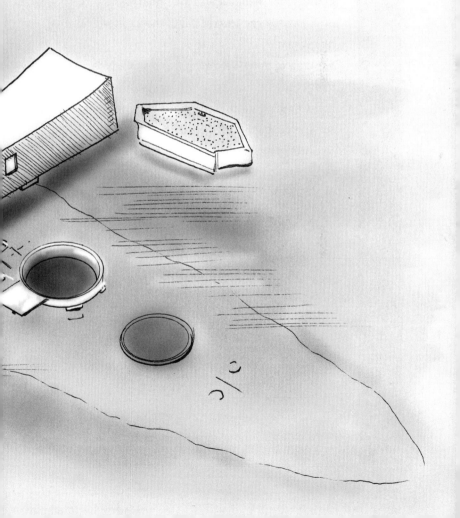

Timeline of the Pearl Harbor Attack—
Morning of December 7, 1941

6:05 — The six Japanese aircraft carriers begin launching planes for the first-wave attack in unison. In fifteen minutes, all 183 planes are in the air.

6:20 — Commander Fuchida gives the signal for his airplanes to head toward Oahu. The flight will take ninety minutes.

6:45 — The crew of the USS *Ward* spot and sink a Japanese midget submarine.

7:00 — Commander Outerbridge reports the sinking of the submarine, but no action is taken.

7:02 — Two army privates on Oahu see a large blip on their radar screen that signals at least fifty incoming planes. Reporting the sighting, the men are told to not worry about it.

7:05 — The second wave of Japanese attack planes is launched from the carriers. By 7:30, a total of 353 Japanese warplanes are in the air, heading toward Pearl Harbor.

7:49 — Fuchida radios his planes, *"To! To! To!"*—the signal to attack.

7:53 — Fuchida sends out the signal *"Tora! Tora! Tora!"* meaning that surprise has been won.

7:55	The Japanese air attack begins at the same time on Pearl Harbor and the US airfields Ewa, Wheeler, Bellows, and Hickam.
8:00	Admiral Kimmel radios his forces, "This is no drill!"
8:05	The *Oklahoma* capsizes with more than four hundred men trapped inside.
8:10	The *Arizona* explodes after a bomb sets off more than a million pounds of gunpowder. The blast kills 1,177 men on the ship.
8:35	The first wave of Japanese airplanes take off.
8:54	The second wave of Japanese airplanes arrives at Oahu, meeting heavy return fire from the Americans.
9:45	The attack is over, one hour and fifty minutes after the first bombs fell. Japanese planes head back to their carriers.

Timeline of World War II

*The key fronts of World War II were Europe and the Pacific.
In this outline, events in the Pacific are italicized.*

Sept 1939	Nazi Germany, under Adolf Hitler, invades Poland. England and France declare war on Germany, thus starting World War II.
June 1940	Germany occupies France. Italy, under dictator Benito Mussolini, supports Germany in declaring war on England and France. *Japanese troops invade Indochina.*
Sept 1940	Germany begins nightly bombings of England. Germany, Italy, and Japan sign an agreement called the Tripartite Pact. It makes them allies against their common enemies, England and France.
July 1941	The United States freezes Japanese financial assets, stopping all oil exports to Japan.
Nov 1941	*Six Japanese aircraft carriers, with hundreds of warplanes aboard, head toward Pearl Harbor.*
Dec 1941	*The Japanese spring a surprise air attack on Pearl Harbor, killing 2,400 Americans. The United States declares war on Japan and enters World War II on the side of the Allies.*
Jan 1942	*Japan overtakes Manila, Philippines.*
Feb 1942	*Japan overtakes Java and the Dutch East Indies.*

April 1942	*In the Philippines, 5,200 captured Americans die in a forced march by the Japanese.*
June 1942	*The US Navy defeats the Japanese at the Battle of Midway, marking a turning point in the Pacific War.*
Sept 1943	Italy surrenders, but Germany continues fighting.
Aug 1944	The French and American armies liberate Paris.
Jan 1945	American troops turn back the Germans in the Battle of the Bulge, the largest land battle in America's history.
Mar 1945	*American troops bomb Tokyo, killing more than eighty thousand people.*
Apr 1945	American soldiers free thirty-two thousand survivors held in Nazi concentration camps. The Nazis killed six million Jews during the war in what is now known as the Holocaust. Adolf Hitler commits suicide.
May 1945	Germany surrenders.
Aug 1945	*The United States drops atomic bombs on Hiroshima (August 6) and Nagasaki (August 9).*
Sept 1945	Japan surrenders.

Bibliography

*Books for young readers

*Allen, Thomas B. *Remember Pearl Harbor: American and Japanese Survivors Tell Their Stories*. Washington, DC: National Geographic Society, 2001.

Bowen, James K. "Pearl Harbor: 7 December 1941." Accessed July 22, 2012. http://www.pacificwar.org.au/pearl_harbor.html.

*Dougherty, Steve. *Pearl Harbor: The U.S. Enters World War II*. New York: Scholastic, 2010.

Fuchida, Captain Mitsuo. "I Led the Air Attack on Pearl Harbor." From *U.S. Naval Institute*. Accessed July 22, 2012. http://www.usni.org.

Jasper, Joy Waldron, James P. Delgado, and Jim Adams. *The USS Arizona*. New York: St. Martin's Press, 2001.

Lord, Walter. *Day of Infamy*. New York: Henry Holt and Company, 1957.

Pearl Harbor: Legacy of Attack. Writer: Patrick Prentice. National Geographic Video, 2001.

*Rice, Earle, Jr. *The Bombing of Pearl Harbor*. San Diego: Lucent Books, 2001.

Stille, Mark E. *Tora! Tora! Tora! Pearl Harbor 1941*. Oxford: Osprey Publishing, 2011.